STEM *trailblazer* BIOS

ANIMAL SCIENTIST AND ACTIVIST JANE GOODALL

DOUGLAS HUSTAD

Lerner Publications ◆ Minneapolis

Lerner Publications Company
A division of Lerner Publishing Group, Inc.
241 First Avenue North
Minneapolis, MN 55401 U.S.A.

For reading levels and more information, look up this title at www.lernerbooks.com.

Content Consultant: Kevin D. Hunt, Professor, Anthropology Department, Director, Human Origins and Primate Evolution Lab, Indiana University

Library of Congress Cataloging-in-Publication Data

Names: Hustad, Douglas.
Title: Animal scientist and activist Jane Goodall / by Douglas Hustad.
Description: Minneapolis : Lerner Publications, 2017. | Includes bibliographical references and index.
Identifiers: LCCN 2015047634 (print) | LCCN 2015049187 (ebook) | ISBN 9781512407884
    (librarybound : alkaline paper) | ISBN 9781512413090 (paperback : alkaline paper) |
    ISBN 9781512410914 (eb pdf)
Subjects: LCSH: Goodall, Jane, 1934—Juvenile literature. | Primatologists—England—Biography—
    Juvenile literature. | Women primatologists—England—Biography—Juvenile literature. |
    Chimpanzees—Tanzania—Gombe Stream National Park—Juvenile literature. | Chimpanzees—
    Research—Juvenile literature. | Conservationists—England—Biography—Juvenile literature. |
    Political activists—England—Biography—Juvenile literature.
Classification: LCC QL31.G58 H87 2017 (print) | LCC QL31.G58 (ebook) | DDC 599.8092—dc23

LC record available at http://lccn.loc.gov/2015047634

Manufactured in the United States of America
1 – PC – 7/15/16

The images in this book are used with the permission of: © Everett Collection Inc/Alamy Stock Photo, p. 4; © Everett Collection Historical/Alamy Stock Photo, p. 6; © Smithsonian Institution Archives/Image #SIA-SIA2008-5175, p. 8; © Josef Friedhuber/iStock.com, p. 10; © Vincent_St_Thomas/iStock.com, p. 11; © Bruce Coleman Inc./Alamy Stock Photo, p. 14; © MHGALLERY/iStock.com, p. 15, p. 20; © Stephen Robinson/NHPA/Photoshot/Newscom, p. 16; © Robert Gray/Getty Image News/Thinkstock, p. 17; © ITV/REX/Newscom, p. 19; © Shikhar Bhattarai/iStock.com, p. 22; © Brian Cahn/ZumaPress/Newscom, p. 25; © Alpha/ZumaPress/Newscom, p. 26; © EdStock/iStock.com, p. 27; © Steve Jurvetson CC2.0, p. 28.

Front Cover: © Michel Gunther/Science Source

CONTENTS

Jane's passion for working with chimps stemmed from an early love of all animals.

AN EARLY LOVE OF ANIMALS

Jane Goodall has been fascinated by animals her entire life. Even before she could walk, she wanted to observe and learn about them. When she was one year old, her father bought her a stuffed **chimpanzee**. Family friends believed the

toy would scare young Jane. But instead, it was the start of a lifelong bond with animals. Jane named her stuffed animal Jubilee, and the chimp still sits on her dresser.

Jane has always been ready and willing to travel to the ends of the earth to see animals. When she was a little girl in England, the first step she took toward studying animals was venturing from her family's farm to the henhouse. One time, she watched one of the hens lay an egg for hours. She was gone so long her family was worried. They even called the police. But Jane was safe and sound. She was utterly fascinated by the miracle of life. Her parents were not upset with her. Instead, they listened intently as she retold the tale.

DREAMING OF AFRICA

Jane had wanted to go to Africa ever since reading about it in her favorite books. She wanted to live with animals, similar to the character in *Tarzan.* She loved stories about Dr. Doolittle, a fictional doctor who talked to animals in Africa. Walking and talking with the animals seemed like an impossible fantasy, but Jane was determined to make it happen. Her mother told her that she could do whatever she put her mind to.

Jane finished high school in 1952. Unfortunately, her family could not afford to send her to college. But she kept studying

Jane was determined to one day with work with animals.

animals on her own. She read and took trips to the Natural History Museum in London, England, to learn all she could. She began work as a secretary at Oxford University. Later, she worked for a **documentary** filmmaker. None of it got her any closer to Africa. So she happily quit when she got the opportunity of a lifetime.

In 1956, a friend invited Jane to her family's farm in Kenya. Jane saw amazing things and met incredible people while there in 1957. One man in particular would change her life. Dr. Louis Leakey was an **archaeologist** and **paleontologist** for the Coryndon Museum in Nairobi, Kenya. Learning of Jane's interest in studying animals, Leakey hired her as a secretary.

THE DREAM COMES TRUE

Goodall began working for Leakey right away. Though she was hired as a secretary, she told him of her desire to make a difference in science. Leakey allowed her to join him and his wife in their search for **fossils**. Even though Goodall had no degree or formal education, she was passionate about animals. She had studied on her own for years. Fossils did not thrill Goodall, but she was inspired just being in Africa. For each fossil she held, she could picture the animal it belonged to.

Leakey thought Goodall would be the perfect person to take on a study of chimpanzees in the wild. He wanted someone who knew about animals, but who did not have formal training. Goodall would be able to observe the animals in her own way, unbiased from previous approaches to animal behavior. Little was known about chimps at the time, and Leakey believed that

Louis Leakey (*right*) and his wife Mary (*left*) were excavating at Olduvai Gorge.

TECH TALK

TECH TALK

"[Leakey] didn't know back then quite how close biologically they [chimpanzees] actually are to us, but it was known they were close. And so he argued that if somebody would go and learn about them in the wild, if we found behavior that was the same or very similar in chimpanzees today and humans today, then if we agreed that there was a common ancestor about six, seven million years ago, then maybe that behavior was present in the common ancestor."

—*Jane Goodall, on Leakey's work*

learning more about them would help people understand their relationship to humans. Goodall enthusiastically accepted the job.

She returned to England in 1959 to prepare to move to Africa full-time. It took more than a year to gather the money for her trip. But by 1960, Goodall was on her way to Africa, this time for good.

Chapter 2

Chimpanzees at Gombe Stream groom each other.

FIRST WORK IN AFRICA

In the summer of 1960, Goodall arrived in Tanganyika. Later called Tanzania, the country was ruled by the United Kingdom at that time. The British government told her that it was not safe there for a young woman traveling alone.

They insisted that she bring a companion. So she brought her mother along. Goodall did not bring much else with her. She had a notebook and a pair of binoculars. She also had a passion for the work.

Goodall set up her research center in Gombe Stream Chimpanzee Reserve near the shores of Lake Tanganyika. She saw a chimp on her very first day of work. But it was only a brief look. The chimps ran away when she got close. But as Goodall spent more time there, they got used to her. It took

Goodall soon observed chimps using sticks to gather food.

months until one chimp felt comfortable enough to approach her. She named him David Greybeard, for his silver whiskers.

As she got closer to the apes, Goodall learned more about them. What she learned challenged everything scientists thought they knew. For one thing, it was thought that only humans used tools. But chimpanzees were not only using tools, they were also making them. The chimps stripped the leaves off of twigs and used them to draw termites out of the ground.

Goodall's discovery redefined what it meant to be human. Tool-making was no longer what separated humans from animals. New criteria would have to be developed. It came as no surprise to Goodall, who knew how intelligent chimps were. But this discovery put her on the scientific map.

METHOD OF STUDY

It was not only Goodall's discoveries that were noteworthy. It was the way she went about them. She was the first to study chimps as individuals. She treated them as people, with their own behavior and personalities. This method felt natural to her. Goodall had no formal training in scientific study. But from what she knew of chimps, she knew what would be the best way to study them.

TECH TALK

"You cannot share your life in a meaningful way with any kind of animal with a reasonably well-developed brain and not realize that animals have personalities."

—Jane Goodall, on her research

In 1962, Leakey helped Goodall get in to Cambridge University in England. She enrolled in a PhD program for ethology. At first Goodall was not even sure what ethology was. But it was what she had already been doing: studying behavior. When Goodall started at Cambridge, she had been studying chimpanzees for fifteen months. Unfortunately that meant little to the scholars at Cambridge.

The scholars at Cambridge felt it was wrong to give animals names instead of numbers. They believed it forced human traits on them and clouded research. But Goodall had known animals all her life, and she knew they had their own personalities. It was this approach that was key to her discoveries.

She brought her supervisor from Cambridge to Africa. He saw firsthand the complex behavior of the chimps.

Goodall closely observes a young chimp at Gombe Stream.

Old-fashioned scientific thinking could not explain it. Goodall's approach of careful observation helped humans understand chimpanzee behavior.

In 1961, the National Geographic Society began funding Goodall's work. In 1963, photographers and writers from

National Geographic magazine traveled to Africa to see the work she was doing. That year the magazine also published the first of Goodall's many articles, "My Life among Wild Chimpanzees."

In 1965, the Society paid for the construction of the Gombe Stream Research Center on the previously empty site where Goodall had been working. It was a full-scale laboratory for scientific work. After four years of traveling back and forth from Africa to England, Goodall was awarded her PhD in ethology in 1966. It was proof that other scholars agreed on the scientific value of her methods.

The Gombe Stream Research Center provides a space for chimpanzee research.

Chapter 3

It took a while for the chimps to get comfortable with Goodall.

RESEARCH AT GOMBE STREAM

Goodall had worked at Gombe since 1960. But with National Geographic's funding, it had become a world-famous center for chimpanzee research by the late 1960s. Students came to Tanzania from all over the globe to learn. Many of the people who came to study at Gombe became famous scientists themselves.

The center became important for everyday people as well. Through books, articles, and television programs, people could see chimpanzees in the wild for the first time. Demonstrating the link between chimps and humans showed how important it was to study their behavior.

There were challenges, too. In 1966, a mysterious disease broke out among the chimps. Six of them either died or disappeared. In 1968, five more chimps disappeared during another outbreak. Among them was David Greybeard. With these setbacks, Goodall learned a lot about how diseases spread. This too was helpful for humans.

Although there were setbacks in the research in the late 1960s, Goodall learned a lot about the animals during this time.

In 1971, Goodall published *In the Shadow of Man*, a book about her time at Gombe up to that point. It was one of the first studies of animals to be read by the general public as well as scientists. Her writing was not dry and scientific. It became a best seller.

THE CHIMP WAR

In 1974, Goodall and her team observed something never seen before. They had already seen chimps eating meat, after previously thinking they were vegetarians. But now they saw chimps killing other chimps for food.

For four years, the chimps waged war on each other. They invaded enemy territory almost as a human military would. It was brutal, but their behavior shed light on how chimps think and behave.

It was hard to tell what caused it. But Goodall traced the start of the war to the death of one of the group's leaders. Other chimps challenged each other for leadership, with some picking sides. This closely matched how human societies behave in a crisis.

By 1975, humans in Tanzania were causing violence too. Foreign researchers were kidnapped. It became a dangerous place to visit, and fewer people came to Gombe. It was not

Goodall's 1971 book brought the lives of chimps into public view.

A chimpanzee communicates with other chimps using a call.

safe for foreigners, including Goodall, who could not work without a military escort. But Tanzanians stepped in to make sure the research could continue. Only one day's worth of data was missed due to the kidnapping.

TECH TALK

"Chimpanzees . . . have been living for hundreds of thousands of years in their forest . . . never overpopulating, never destroying the forest. I would say that they have been in a way more successful than us as far as being in harmony with the environment."

—Jane Goodall, on chimpanzee habits

Goodall brings a stuffed chimp to speaking events, including in Nepal in November 2012.

BECOMING AN ACTIVIST

Goodall founded the Jane Goodall Institute in 1977. It funded further research at Gombe Stream. But the goal of the institute was not just to help chimps in Africa. It also raised awareness around the world about the importance of protecting chimps and other wildlife. The institute now has dozens of chapters in many countries.

Goodall started to spend less time at Gombe Stream in the 1970s and 1980s. Between 1970 and 1975, she was a part-time professor in California. In 1973, she became a visiting professor at the University of Dar es Salaam in Tanzania. She has held that position for more than forty years. In 1986, Goodall attended a conference about endangered chimps in the wild. She began to devote her time to educating people about the dangers these animals faced.

At this point, Goodall began to spend more time working to protect chimpanzees than studying them in the wild.

TECH TALK

"Understanding, spending time learning about and thinking about the consequences of the little choices we make each day, and how they will affect the environment, how they will affect animals and the human community. And this does lead to small changes in our behavior, because I have seen it again and again."

—*Jane Goodall, on the future of conservation*

She began work as an activist and **conservationist**. Even at Gombe, the surrounding area faced deforestation. The chimps' habitat was shrinking. And they faced new and dangerous diseases. It was important to not only save the chimps, but also to continue to study them as well.

INVOLVING YOUNG PEOPLE

Goodall believed the future of conservation was in the hands of young people. In 1991, she founded the Roots & Shoots program. It began with a handful of students from Tanzania. Hundreds of thousands of young people from more than 130 countries now participate in the program.

Goodall started the program because, in her travels, she met young people who wanted to protect the environment but didn't know how. In countries all over the world, the program helps kids get together and work on projects toward that goal.

Roots & Shoots is involved in many causes, using science to make the world a better place. Groups plant trees and protect clean water. Students everywhere are able to participate whether they have any science education or not. Roots & Shoots helps the next generation use science and technology for conservation.

Day of Peace

Goodall speaks with students at a Roots & Shoots event in Los Angeles, California, in 2007.

NEW CAUSES AND THE FUTURE

Since 1986, Goodall has never been in the same place for more than three weeks. She travels approximately 300 days per year. She has received numerous awards for her work. In 2004, she received the title of Dame Jane Goodall from Queen

Goodall was made a Dame of the Order of the British Empire in 2004.

Goodall has dedicated her life to helping animals and the environment.

Elizabeth II of the United Kingdom. This honor is given to British people for service to their country. In Goodall's case, it was her scientific breakthroughs.

In her speeches, Goodall encourages people to take action to protect the planet.

Goodall saw many of the problems facing the globe for herself in Tanzania. Deforestation, cruelty to animals, and climate change are some of these problems. Instead of just observing, Goodall now helps others take action.

She continues to educate people on problems facing animals and the environment. It is her belief that when people get together to solve problems, they can influence anything.

TIMELINE

1934

Jane Goodall is born in London.

1952

Goodall graduates from high school and begins working for a documentary filmmaker.

1957

Goodall visits Africa and meets Louis Leakey, who offers her a job.

1960

Goodall moves to Tanganyika to study chimpanzees.

1961

Goodall observes chimps using tools and eating meat, behavior never seen before.

1962

Goodall begins studying at Cambridge University and defends her scientific research methods.

1965

Goodall earns her PhD in ethology and the Gombe Stream Research Center is built.

1977

The Jane Goodall Institute is founded.

1986

Goodall leaves Gombe Stream and begins her activism career.

SOURCE NOTES

9   Academy of Achievement, "Jane Goodall Interview: The Great Conservationist," last modified July 6, 2009, http://www.achievement.org/autodoc/page/goo1int-1.

13 David Quammen, "Being Jane Goodall," *National Geographic*, October 2010, http://ngm.nationalgeographic.com/2010/10/jane-goodall/quammen-text.

20 Biography.com, "Jane Goodall Biography," http://www.biography.com/people/jane-goodall-9542363.

23 Academy of Achievement, "Jane Goodall Interview: The Great Conservationist."

GLOSSARY

archaeologist
a person who studies people and cultures that lived a long time ago

chimpanzee
an ape known for its high intelligence and humanlike behavior

conservationist
someone who works to protect animals, plants, and natural resources

documentary
a type of movie featuring real-life news stories

fossils
bones, shells, or other parts of an animal or plant, preserved as rock

paleontologist
a person who studies things that lived a long time ago

FURTHER INFORMATION

BOOKS

Goodall, Jane. *My Life with the Chimpanzees*. New York: Pocket Books, 1996. Check out Jane Goodall's book describing her interest in animals and early work in Tanzania.

Shepherd, Jodie. *Jane Goodall*. New York: Children's Press, 2015. This book discusses Jane Goodall's groundbreaking work with chimpanzees.

Silvey, Anita. *Untamed: The Wild Life of Jane Goodall*. Washington, DC: National Geographic, 2015. Learn more about specific chimpanzees Jane Goodall worked with, and how her work changed peoples' understanding of these animals.

WEBSITES

The Jane Goodall Institute
http://www.janegoodall.org
Learn more about chimpanzees and their habitats, while also learning how to get involved.

Jane Goodall's Roots & Shoots Program
http://www.janegoodall.org/what-we-do/roots-and-shoots
Find projects to work on and other ways to help your community through Jane Goodall's Roots & Shoots program.

National Geographic: Jane Goodall
http://www.nationalgeographic.com/explorers/bios/jane-goodall
Discover more about Jane Goodall's background, past work, and current activist efforts.

LERNER

SOURCE

Expand learning beyond the printed book. Download free, complementary educational resources for this book from our website, www.lerneresource.com.

INDEX

ABOUT THE AUTHOR

Douglas Hustad is a children's author who has written several books on science and technology for young people. Originally from northern Minnesota, he now lives in San Francisco with his wife.